D0532360

deadline*!
ironing
take biscuit out of coffee before it melts
invoice Pan
2lbs potatoes
Northern Ireland
layout spreads
Viv Quillin
Life as we know it

Taking the Lid off Kids

Written and Illustrated by Viv Quillin

A Pan Original
Pan Books
London and Sydney

First published 1983 by Pan Books Ltd,
Cavaye Place, London SW10 9PG

ISBN 0 330 28070 8

Printed and bound by Collins, Glasgow.

Fizzics
this book is dedicated to my 3 lovely kids. P.S. whose turn is it to wash up?

Does not suffer from any of the following

- : bedwetting
- : stammering
- : dandruff
- : occasional puddles
- : nail biting
- : thumb sucking
- : nightmares

ccccc CREEP

Doggies
Love
Them

Regards half-chewed rusks and dog biscuits as collectors' items. Moves on to save cut-out-and-glue zoo on back of cereal packets, goes off cereal with eighteen cartons left in larder, untouched except for holes cut out of backs.

Hoards second hand chewing gum, decaying sweets, broken Dinky cars and dead birds.

Aquires vast wealth in later life by selling old rubbish for extremely large amounts of money.

BALLET MAD

Comes in wide variety of shapes and sizes. Requires devoted seamstress/valet/chauffeur for shepherding it to frequent dance classes and witnessing prolonged displays of its agility.

Smashes quite a lot of things whilst practising grands jetés in lounge.

brownie

Knits a mean dishcloth and polishes people's slippers without having to be asked. Won't eat anything that hasn't been toasted over an open fire, but does a good deed every day without mercy. Always finds way home no matter where it's left.

Leans towards missionary work, armed forces or anything else involving strenuous discipline and a uniform.

wakey, wakey
rise and shine!

CANNIBAL

Only a masochist will attempt to breast feed it, as this type would send a Pirahna screaming for help.

It quickly realises cot bars and table legs are not edible and moves onto living flesh, as found on parents and pets.

Other siblings move out or (more commonly) cease washing to promote a distasteful flavour.

Enid Blytun
stinks

Creative

Draws all the time, finding expensive wallpaper particuarly satisfying to work on. Young Henry Moores can sometimes be persuaded to build structures out of flour paste and egg boxes.

Usually prefers bold visual statements after the style of Andy Warhol and/or Jackson Pollock.

Becomes rich, trendy artist or gets fined a lot for obscene graffitti, depending on social climate.

DAMPROOF

Heavily draped with super-absorbant padding, double glazed from waist to knee in plastic sheeting with storm proof elastic.

Nobody but the nappy changer knows the full horror of what lurks underneath.

People like this, end up running the country.

gasp
coff
phew
kills

emonstrative

Always ready for a cuddle, it's little arms have a vice-like grip. When prised off with crowbar it immediatly re-attaches itself to a different bit of the object of affection.

Useful foot warmer in cold weather, also brings a new dimension to bondage games

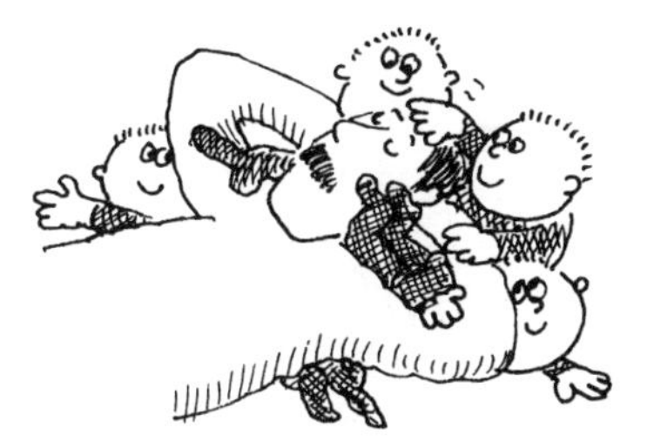

ENGINEER (embroyonic)

Works on the principal that one must destroy in order to rebuild.

Dismantles cot at eight months and progresses to reconstructing stereo, foundations of house and anything else supposedly out of reach. Handcuffs may help to contain this child.

Welded on.

to get at the
car burettor, simply
remove
the
?
KASTROL
EXTRA

REQUEST STOP
DESPARAT
DAN
CENTRE
FOLD.

Exhibitionist

Early signs include stripping off on supermarket floor, and striding downstairs at dinner parties - naked below the waist - asking who would like to wipe it's bottom.

If not nipped in bud, moves on to charging threepence a look behind the playgroup toilets.

Could have a future in films.

Lies all the time.

Wakes parents up to look for horse under bed at 3 am, and tells complete fabrications about friends which lead it's parents to fall out with theirs.

At seven years it's running the school magazine, "Taking The Lid Off Primary School," and handling its first libel suit.

Becomes famous novelist/chat show personality.

3 BILLION
BED
TIME
TALES

Fun loving

Prolongs bed time indefinitely with merry games and pleas for one more story. Tends to jump on people from top of doors and also likes putting dead suprises in guest bed. Reaches peak efficiency around two a.m.

A really dedicated fun lover can shorten parents life expectancy by at least twenty years.

Knows how to mix a stiff drink and when to keep quiet. Hobbies include eating vegetables and reading to itself in silence.

Agrees with parents a lot; is generally loathed by siblings.

FINAL DEMAND
Giant Lego Set
Racing trike
Electric teddy bear. £19.59.
Automatic Action man. £32.99
PTO

Instinctively knows the best and rejects anything else. Screams if bottle is not at room temperature or nipple oversalted.

Expects food to look attractive and doesn't hesitate to re-arrange on floor or in hair if not satisfied. Willing to experiment with new tastes such as boot polish or cat's dinner.

Later, gives parents recipes for diluted cabbage and sliced custard, straight from dinner lady's own lips.

HELPFUL

Likes making grey and sweaty pastry which tastes like cardboard and involves expensive bridgework for those foolhardy enough to set teeth into it.

Keen assistant in garage, discovering long-lost useful tins of black, runny stuff, when it accidentally kicks them over. Sometimes burns down house whilst making surprise cup of tea for parents.

Biscuits

When they've thundered through house, dust takes half an hour to settle, carpet never recovers. Week's biscuit supply is reduced to handful of crumbs in minutes.

When playing fifteen-a-side football there are still kids left over, these fight in flower beds until called on to replace injured.

Can be of real help when moving house, even better - skip the help and move without forwarding address.

INCONTINENT

Rushes to loo every ten minutes in case it gets caught with knickers up. Has potty shaped groove on bottom due to misguided theory "It can't hold on forever."

Carpets are dotted with clean patches where scattered showers and occasionally worse have been sponged/scraped off. Parents have squatters' rights in launderette.

Condition takes at least two years to clear up and some of the marks never come out.

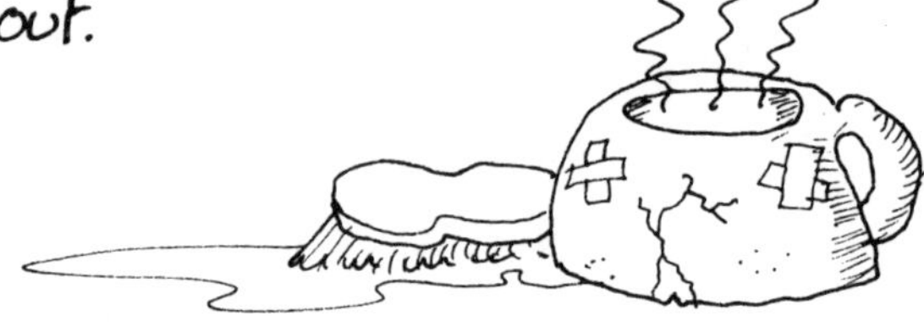

and after that
told her not to
– know they shouldn't
then they went and
thought you ought to
know
DAILY GRASS

Informer

Tells who pushed it down the waste disposal / hid Dresden remains in laundry basket / added weed killer to cat's milk.

A useful aid to adults who like to know if their PILLS have been swopped for aspirin, and which child is lighting secret bonfires under the stairs.

Parents call this sort of kid a Responsible Person, the informed on call it something else.

JEALOUS

Cuddles the new baby with tenderness of a raging annaconda, also offers to push pram across road when pedestrian light is red. Insists on recount after cornflakes have been dished up, and whips out stop watch when other siblings get a brief look in.

Sleeps between parents because it's not letting them have anything it can't share.

skaters
waltz

Jet propelled

Parent leaves it gurgling quietly in carry-cot and trips over it two minutes later at bottom of garden. With dusters sewn onto extremities, it keeps parquet floors like mirrors when it learns to crawl.

Never runs when it could sprint and leaves trail of grounded people in it's wake; good at exercising dogs, other people's patience and delivering letters abroad when you can't wait for the post. to do it.

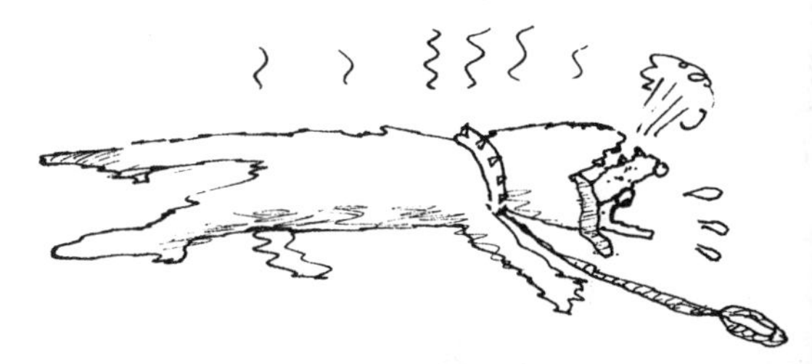

ARATE KID

Wears white pyjama bottoms and a loose jacket which either strains to meet at the front or wraps round twice according to build of wearer.

Often, only knee high to a golliwog, but can tie bows in kids three times its own size. This is equally character building for thrower and throwee. May have trouble getting it to do homework once it's got the trick of hurling parents over shoulder.

Kiddy

Tap dances in shoes with large satin bows on, and has repertoire Shirley Temple routines which it performs at a moment's un-notice whilst parents block exits.

Leaps up to help conjuror at children's parties, spotting the trick loudly and ruining show; kiddies cannot be held responsible for their behaviour, they are a product of whimsical adults.

Leader

Easily picked out by troop of subordinates either driven in front with stout stick or dragged behind, tied with washing line.

Every body wants to be on it's side at games to avoid being kicked in as an opponent. Any member of the gang would lay down their life for the leader and may do so whilst testing out branches, drain pipes and twelve foot fences to see if it's safe for the boss

Becomes Head Prefect or Mr/Ms Big of school mafia.

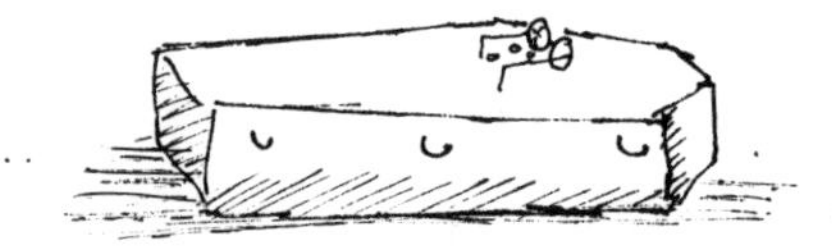

OK guys
re-route to
plan B
up

CHEAPOBIX
the lowbudget
cereal for
kids

low budget

Sleeps in cutlery drawer when first born, later moves in with dog, (no longer requiring blankets if dog is big and hairy.) Travel sick in well sprung pram, prefers to hitch hike.

Eats table scraps, things in garden and snacks from dog bowl; Hates big toys but likes cardboard boxes they arrived in.

Plans to live in old car and be professional vagrant when it grows up.

MOTHERLY

Stuffs cat into Babygro and wheels it out in pram, firmly strapped down to stop it falling out/escaping. Sponges visitors' hands and faces after meals.

Takes over Wendy house at playgroup, frantically bandaging other kids and putting them to bed, between straightening the place up before it's time to go home. Talks with hands on hips, and harrassed voice is sometimes recognised by parent as perfect imitation of their own.

I haven't got all day now EAT YOUR GREENS

– what was that Mavis?

Mythical

Always found in books on child raising. Goes four hours between feeds and sleeps through the night from three weeks. It also cries for a reason, (which is listed in the child raising books.)

Grows into the sunny child with symmetrical freckles and well brushed teeth, seen in telly commercials; wears an ultra-white T-shirt that comes clean in the wash – another myth.

Although some people feel kids are grossly misrepresented, without such romantic illusions, the species could easily die out.

NEVER MISSES ANYTHING

Eyes have 360° swivel range and ears gently flap even when asleep. Asks questions like, "Why does Daddy only wear aftershave when he's going to work late?" and "Did you know you've put a bracelet in your bag Mummy?" (in middle of Harrods)

When parents inevitably split up, it reports to mother that Daddy's friend has her own toothbrush in the bathroom and remarks to father that the label on Mummy's new shoes said £27·50p. This leads to adultery proceedings and maintenance being halved, in one stroke.

Becomes private eye or front-room-curtain-twitcher.

I've never seen you put perfume on your chest before, Mummy
I SPY
WEEKLY
LUST 5
Dinners in Oven dear, don't wait up.

Newborn

Scrawny, red and wrinkled, rather like an elderly testicle. Deafeningly loud, doubly incontinent, self centred, and totally helpless.

Within hours of it's arrival, the whole household is turned upside-down trying to guess and carry out its slightest whim.

Instincts speak louder than words.

Outdoor

Beats cat in sprint out to garden at first light. Has rosy cheeks deepening to mauve in winter, is inseparable from wellies.

Permanent row of duffel coats, socks and woolly undies gently steam on radiators. Axminster has long since vanished under sea of mud and Trodden In Things.

May develop into keen gardener but more often wants to excavate old ruins beginning with own house.

OTHER PEOPLE'S KIDS
Have all sorts of nasty little vices quite unknown to one's own kids
FAT.
PRECOCIOUS SHOW OFF
blah
blah
ODD
VICIOUS BULLY
SPOILT
BRAT

OWN KIDS
which have had the benefit of expert upbringing.
STURDY
MATURE FOR AGE
blah
blah
HIGHLY INDIVIDUAL
LEADER
SENSITIVE

Birmingham
42 miles

PLACID

Doesn't mind being bathed in stone cold water by slow, inexperienced parents, and enjoys lying on back staring at sky or ceiling for long periods.

Gets left outside shops and pubs a lot as parents keep forgetting they've got it; either walks home alone or waits to be collected if it's strapped in pram.

Won't panic if house burns down, but watches telly quietly until firemen carry them both out.

Prober

Affects all ages but grown ups do it discreetly behind the paper. This child has an uncanny awareness of when it's being watched and instantly rams a finger in to an eye bulging degree.

Can be found dead centre in every family photograph, particuarly weddings, discovering previously unexplored regions. Home territory is liberally dotted with stickers.

A really dedicated prober should have hands strapped down if there is any possibility of head caving in.

such a
mild little
chap..

UIET

Dismantles washing machine and empties kitchen cupboard into resulting flood without a sound. NEVER trust this child when it's not making a noise.

Absorbs intimate family scandals and personal revelations, sitting silently behind sofa unravelling carpet, then gently repeats the most indiscreet bits during a shocked silence at the tea-table.

When older, mixes inconspicuously with the famous, then blackmails them.

uins

Morning feed is mixed in a bucket and dished up with a shovel; post meal wind force can reach hurricane levels.

Nappy washing is on par with painting Forth bridge and some quin-owners just leave kids in the bath until puberty.

On plus side, they can be hired out for advertising gripe water, or featured in articles so other people can enjoy reading about how easy they've got it with only triplets or twins. With the revenue, parents can pay to have their nervous breakdown privately, or even pay some one else to look after the kids.

they've just had lunch

I'll just take a look –
back in a minute. . . .

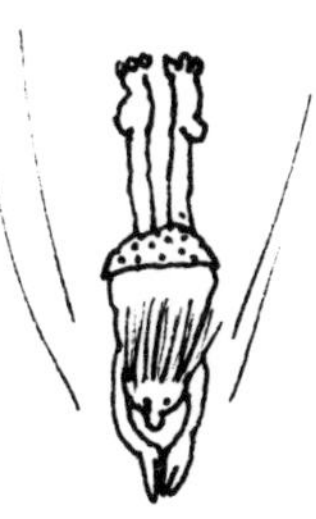

RECKLESS

Expert highboard diver, two years before it learns to swim. Test drives pedal car on M5 and finds it's not unbreakable after all. Saves expense on clothes by being encased in plaster for long periods.

When not in hospital, it is always willing to investigate noises in night whilst rest of family hide under bed.

If it grows up, becomes human cannon ball, lion tamer or secondary school teacher.

Ruthless

Long after other babies have resigned themselves to going to sleep, this one is still bellowing for attention because it never gives in. When on the last stretch home with weeks' groceries and the pushchair's just shed a wheel, it reminds parent about promise to take it swimming after lunch.

Nags mercilessley for sweets before tea, then demands hush money not to tell the other kids.

Goes far in politics and possible destruction of world.

Pay owt
oar else

Shall we have another
double whisky?

going out to
play dear?

STROPPY

Has permanent scowl and wears black eye a lot. Clothes are often untidy ie. sleeve torn out, trousers knotted round neck.

It may take on opponents twice own size and need kitting out with steel toe caps and fishing weights sewn into satchel; if it prefers arguing with small fry, remove sharp objects from its person and keep it in house slippers.

Quarrel some kids who wear horn rimmed specs and spotty bow-ties, may take stroppiness up professionally.

Not to be confused with Super-pain which misquotes uninteresting facts from Readers Digress magazine, but is good for insomnia.

The really bright kid is often found in remedial reading and still needs help with shoelaces in adolescence. Upsets discipline and dignity in class by correcting teacher during introduction to advanced physics.

After several years' incomprehensible research at university, it goes abroad where it's appreciated.

EUREKA!

TENDERLY NURTURED

Every germ is boiled out of bottle, nappies, pram and nursery air; when it starts nursery school it catches everything.

Parents send notes to school asking for it's meat to be cut up small and permission to stay in at break if the temperature drops below 58°. Has electric blanket, thermal underwear and porridge injections in winter and spends summer in shade and pure cotton, quietly sipping chilled drinks.

Always looks sickly and generally out lives grandchildren.

Travels by E-type pram in fun fur matching hat, scarf and gloves set. Hair is naturally straight or curly depending on what's being worn currently on television; rompers by Zandra.

School uniform is daily let out, taken in, raised, lowered or slashed, according to the news from Paris. Clothes are instantly copied by Active Man/Shindy doll for next seasons toys.

This model is expensive to run.

note
punks fasten detail

get me "Tiny smear" productions - big bows and the hanging knicker leg are back....

I like YOU
Coff
gasp

Nose like a stagnant river and produces rag one wouldn't wipe a gear box with, to stem flood; Also suffers with hot plimsolls and clammy hands, (sometimes containing crushed caterpillar.)

Instinctively senses those who find it particularly loathsome and presses up close to them.

Incurable dandruff follows it to the grave.

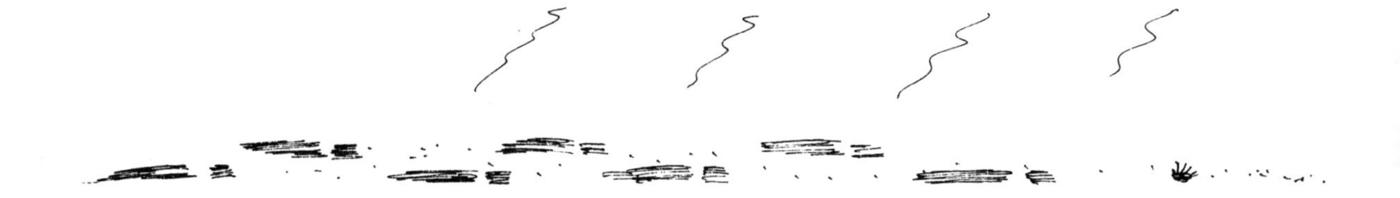

Embroidered, smocked and reared by hand, usually Nanny's; won't touch a dummy if it's not bone china. Wears ermine trimmed cloaks in winter and tweed shorts on either sex during summer holidays in Scotland.

When playing house, its friends find themselves being the under parlour maid or second footman. Often shows fondness for polo mints/sweaters/ponies, and little ginger dogs.

I say Nanny, these Harris Tweed bootees itch quite fearfully

I wanted a
small white
sliced

AGUE

Home territory has sagging ceilings and pervading smell of mildew from baths constantly left running. Never leave this sort to watch the toast.

If it remembers address and returns home, it's forgotton what it went out for in the first place. Loses homework, thread of conversation, and other people's patience.

Sometimes improves with senility.

F. Bloggs
5 Acacia Av
Milton keynes

Victim

The only one on Costa Brava with Galloping-gut-rot the whole fortnight. Trails behind on beach complaining about weight of sun hat; sand gets up it's shorts and sea gets up it's nose. Sun appears briefly on eighth day and it's got sunstroke with delirium by mid-morning.

Feels faint at pantomimes and birthday parties and is sick before dinner and visiting relatives on Christmas day.

Becomes comedian or red-coat at holiday camp.

30p
30p

If we all stole Aston Martins because we liked the colour where would it end?
... seem to have mislaid my purse....

WARD OF COURT

Put on trial before magistrates wearing hairy suits with leather patches and pork pie hats, garlanded with fishing tackle.

The tweed brigade often feel delinquents should be Made An Example Of, so they don't Get Away With It. After the court hearing they retire for a glass of port and reminisce about setting the science lab on fire, or driving the head's car into a wall after eight pints, whilst still in primary school.

These activities are referred to as High Spirited Pranks.

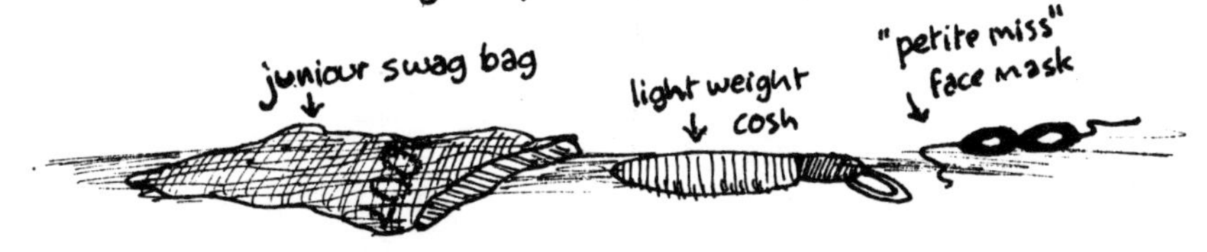

Work shy

Still slumped in heap at bottom of pram when other eight month olds are sitting up scanning the horizon for sweet shops. Won't go up playgroup slide because of too many steps and hides in toilet with "Bedtyme Stories" when it's time to tidy up.

Sleeps standing up which saves making bed, and lives on soup as there's only one piece of cutlery to wash up.

Makes good artist's model or door stop.

Down with
foreigners
WIERDOS
+Freaks
with 2 Legs

XENOPHOBE

Dislikes anybody different to itself, so as cloning is not yet perfected it hates everybody.

This gives it great scope politically and socially. Could be successful in many careers and is frequently revered by those it trod on, on the way up.

mas

Unable to have hospital delivery despite being first baby and mother very young. Average weight, height and apparently carried own lighting system.

May have initiated the original baby shower, attended by foreign officials and sundry shepherds on the night shift.

Studied carpentry for some years but eventually recognised vocation as teacher.

he doesn't half show up the dust Joseph

he was wiv
me all afternoon

ES-MAN

Sucks up to whichever parent is winning argument. Refuses to back up Dad's claim that he was not inebriated when he mowed the lounge carpet, as he's obviously on a loser.

Agrees to help more in kitchen/muck out bathroom/remove toad from loo, and having soothed enraged parent, returns, glazed eyed to telly, without doing anything.

Could have career in politics; specializing in switching to the "in" party.

Youth

Loses curves and dimples overnight and shoots up two feet, making a stick insect look like Mrs Mills in comparison.

Half starved appearance combined with wild hair and grey neck implies parental neglect, when they are in fact, being eaten out of the house and haven't a stitch to their names as it's "borrowed" entire contents of parental wardrobe.

This age is the beginning of the end.

TODAY IS FRIDAY
THE DATE IS 16
THE WEATHER IS Rotten

EALOUS

Delivered by bus conductor on 98B to Hounslow, two weeks before due.

Asks keen, loud questions in shops like, "where do astronauts do their poohs?" First hand to go up in class regardless of whether it knows the answer.

Difficult child to keep up with, but willing parents can learn a lot from it, including where astronauts do their poohs.

Zombie

Totally bored and uninterested in any kind of activity, only coming out of coma very occasionally to check for spots or split ends, otherwise sits unmoving in front of television.

Parents can do spot check to see if it's died by turning t.v. off, if there's no response within five minutes, it probably has.

pack it up
Gran, I'm
watching
telly